First published December 2025
Written by Fran Solly
Illustrated by Robyn Kilgour
Prepared for publication by Lucy Tarin, Seaside Scribbles
Instagram @seaside_scribbles_
Port Lincoln, South Australia 5606

Paperback: ISBN 978-1-7643945-1-2

Marie's long flight is based on the true story of an Osprey chick hatched in 2024 on the artificial nest platform at Coobowie in South Australia.

To learn more about the South Australian Osprey Recovery Program please visit www.friendsofosprey.com.au All profits from the sale of this book will be directed to assist the recovery program.

I would like to sincerely thank Robyn Kilgour for donating her time and skill to illustrate the book – it would not have been possible without her. Thanks also to Dave Wetherall, Bazz Hockaday and David Donovan who generously shared photographs used as the basis for the illustrations.

Special thanks to all those who assisted with Marie's recovery especially Dave Wetherall, Malcolm and Marie Stanton, Peter Sanders and Roy Dennis OBE, MBE without whose skill, knowledge and determination the outcome may have been far different.

Connect with us:

✉ friendsofosprey@gmail.com
f Friends of Osprey Sth Aus

Marie's Long Flight

Written by Fran Solly - Illustrated by Robyn Kilgour

Marie, her mum and dad, and her two sisters, Libby and Missy, lived on a wonderful nest platform specially built for them at Coobowie.

Her mum and dad spent months furnishing the platform with the best sticks, and lining it with soft seaweed.

Marie is a very special Osprey. She was chosen to be part of the Friends of Osprey Recovery Program to help save all the Osprey in her State. When Marie was not quite ready to fly, she was fitted with a satellite tracker that she wore on her back like a backpack. The tracker meant that the Friends of Osprey would be able to see where she flew. Marie also got bracelets for her legs, one red and one white. Missy got red and pink bracelets, and Libby's were silver and pink, but only Marie got the special tracker.

Some weeks went by and the three chicks strengthened their wings with lots of flapping, and occasionally little helicopter jumps.

The day came when Marie was ready to fly.

Missy and Libby watched in amazement
as Marie took to the sky and headed for the beach.

This flying stuff was harder than it looked and Marie crashed into the waves, eventually using her wings to paddle ashore.

She was very sad and sorry for herself.
It was cold and soon got dark, so she was a little bit frightened.

The next morning Marie was cold and hungry,
but some nice men climbed down the cliff and spoke to her.

They told her not to be afraid, they were there to help.
She had seen the men before and knew they were her friends.

Soon, she was carefully carried up the cliff and kept warm so she could
dry her feathers. Best of all, the men fed her some delicious pilchards
and she soon felt much happier.

There was just one problem. There was no way to get Marie back to her nest.

The next day Marie was taken to a new home at Gleesons Landing and now she had a foster mum and dad, a new sister, Annie, and brother, Herbert.

Marie soon came to love her foster mum and dad, and her new family.

She stayed with her foster family,
practicing her flying until she got really good at it.

She could do big circles and land on branches or rocks.

Then, her foster family taught her to fish
by hurtling into the water with talons ready.
She was soon skilled at catching delicious fish that she could eat all by herself.

RK 2025

Eventually Marie knew it was time to find her own beach and her own perch. She wasn't too sure where to go so she flew south right over Kangaroo Island, and way, way down to the continental shelf where she could no longer see any land.

RK 2025

There she met Queenie the Royal Albatross who was soaring high and low over the waves. Queenie flew alongside to chat and said,

"Marie you are a very special Osprey, but you have gone the wrong way, you don't glide over the waves like I do. You must turn back to land."

RK 2025

Before long she saw land again and stopped to fish.

She met Phantom at American Beach,
and saw that she was also a special Osprey with a satellite tracker.

Phantom said, "you can't stop here Marie, this is my home,
and there is no room for you. You must find your own beach."

Marie said farewell and off she flew again, past the big city and further north.

She flew on and on. Sometimes she thought she saw lakes but when she flew down
to them, they were dry. The dry lakes didn't have any fish,
and she hadn't eaten for the longest time, she was really starting to worry.

Marie stopped in a tree near Woomera to rest awhile,
and was joined by Walter and Winnie the Wedge-tailed Eagles.
They chatted and asked why she was there. Walter and Winnie said,

"Marie, you have come too far. There is no food for you here. You must hurry back
to the coast and find somewhere to fish."

Thanking Walter and Winnie, and with their directions, Marie flew south.

— MARIE'S LONG JOURNEY —

Soon Marie could see the sea.
This time she was not going to let it out of her sight.
She had learnt that to fish she must be by the sea.

She stopped awhile near Port Lincoln,
and practiced her fishing skills.

At last, she caught a puffer fish.
It didn't taste very good but she was hungry, so she ate it all up.

After a rest, Marie flew off again,
this time being very careful to follow the coast.
After a few more days of flying she came to an area of long
white sandy beaches. It was sheltered and the water was shallow,
so it was perfect for her to fish.

Marie had found her new forever home at last in the Coffin Bay National Park.

NORTHERN TERRITORY

SOUTH AUSTRALIA

WESTERN AUSTRALIA

NEW SOUTH WALES

VICTORIA

WOOMERA AREA

Lake Dey Dey

Lake Maurice
(Carle thulka)

Ooldea Range

Nullabor Plain

Gawler Ranges

Flinders Ranges

Pt. Augusta

Coffin Bay

Pt. Lincoln

Coobertie

Adelaide

Kangaroo Island

Southern Ocean

— MARIE'S LONG JOURNEY —

Juvenile returning to the nest.

Family at the nest.

Marie swimming.

Marie feeling lost.

www.ingramcontent.com/pod-product-compliance
Lightning Source LLC
Chambersburg PA
CBHW041556030426

42338CB00017B/1619